The Calendar and Beyond

Written by
Kimberly Jordano

Editor: Kim Cernek

Illustrator: Darcy Tom

Cover Illustrator: Mark McIntyre

Designer: Terri Lamadrid

Cover Designer: Barbara Peterson

Art Director: Tom Cochrane

Project Director: Carolea Willi...

D1456716

Table of Contents

Introduction

The Calendar and Beyond offers innovative ideas for expanding one of your most reliable and essential primary-classroom teaching tools—the daily calendar. Learn how to implement a variety of fun, child-centered activities that introduce, provide basic practice with, and review key skills and concepts on a daily basis.

The program outlined in *The Calendar and Beyond* emphasizes a daily routine—a necessity for young students—that adapts to your class as they develop intellectually throughout the year. Use the sample activities in this book as building blocks to customize a program that accommodates your unique teaching style, your curriculum requirements, and the needs of your students. Take students beyond a discussion about the days of the week and implement hands-on activities that encourage them to observe patterns in their world; explore place value, graphing, and telling time; decode and generate new words; and recite poetry.

The repetitive, predictable lessons in this book are designed to promote students' successful learning and increased self-esteem. Over 30 interactive displays that you can create by following detailed, step-by-step directions will attract and hold students' attention and interest. This makes introducing and reinforcing basic skills on a daily basis fun and motivating for you and your students.

Customizing Your Calendar Program

As you read through the activities, select the ones that are the most meaningful for your class or those that can be easily adapted to fit your curriculum. Add and remove activities throughout the year as they become more appropriate for your students' ever-changing developmental needs.

Remember that the calendar isn't just for the morning anymore! This book includes interactive activities designed to meet a variety of daily teaching needs. Choose some lessons to present every morning. Select other activities that are perfect for transitional times and teachable moments. Implement new activities for the end of the day or for homework. Use the following descriptions to help you plan which activities to use when in your daily schedule.

This Is the Way We Start Our Day

Use the activities in this section as the staples of your daily calendar. Invite your class to sit with you by the calendar first thing every day to say hello and to "warm up" for another busy day of learning. Because these lessons are so predictable, they are never too demanding and are always a lot of fun.

This Will Only Take a Minute

Use the math and language activities in this section as mini-lessons throughout the day or to fill those impromptu, teachable moments. These lessons are also great for introducing new skills or reviewing old ones.

Before We Say Good-Bye

Those last few minutes before the bell rings are the perfect time to use the calendar to review what students learned that day. Use the activities in this section to ensure that students have something interesting and meaningful to share with an eager parent who asks "What did you do today?"

Now-and-Then Activities

Students will enjoy these activities whether you include them on a daily basis or only now and again. Each activity features an important skill that is easy to learn in a lesson or two but is always exciting to revisit every so often.

You CAN Take It with You

This section shows you how to make adorable, durable learning kits that coordinate with your calendar activities. These kits give students an opportunity to practice essential math and language arts skills at home. These activities strengthen the home–school connection and let students share with family members some of the exciting things they are doing in your class.

Getting Started

Once you've had a chance to review the activities and decide which ones you want to implement in your classroom, make a sketch of everything you want to display on and with your calendar. Think about how to arrange all the pieces of your calendar in an organized, inviting display. Pages 6–7 feature a visual reference of all the calendar components described in this book.

Use colorful decoratives in your displays to attract and maintain student interest. Laminate each piece so you can reuse your displays year after year. The goal of this approach to using the calendar is to get students actively involved in their own learning, so it is important to include pieces that students can manipulate on their own. Place your finished calendar display in an area where the whole class can comfortably sit and see it with an unobstructed view.

Decide which parts of the calendar you want to address first thing each morning and which are best suited for other times in the day. As you make your calendar the focal point of your classroom and your students become familiar with their daily routine, they will start to demonstrate knowledge and skills beyond those you intended to teach!

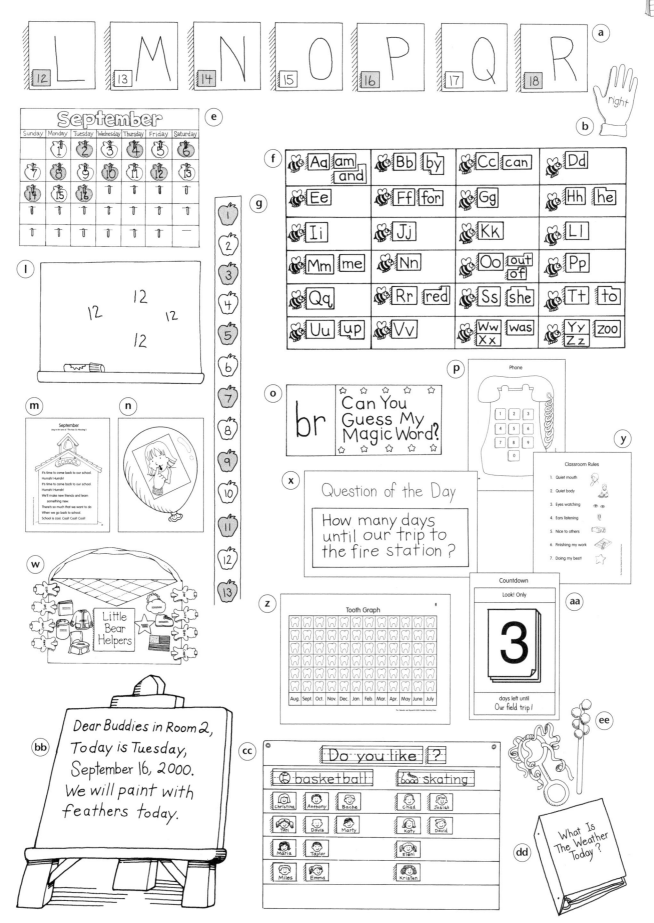

(a)

L (12) M (13) N (14) O (15) P (16) Q (17) R (18)

(b) right

(e) September

Sunday	Monday	Tuesday	Wednesday	Thursday	Friday	Saturday
	1	2	3	4	5	6
7	8	9	10	11	12	13
14	15	16				
						—

(f)
Aa am and	Bb by	Cc can	Dd
Ee	Ff for	Gg	Hh he
Ii	Jj	Kk	Ll
Mm me	Nn	Oo out of	Pp
Qq	Rr red	Ss she	Tt to
Uu up	Vv	Ww Xx was	Yy Zz zoo

(g)

(l)
12
12
12
12

(m) September

It's time to come back to our school.
Hurrah! Hurrah!
It's time to come back to our school.
Hurrah! Hurrah!
We'll make new friends and learn something new.
There's so much that we want to do
When we go back to school.
School is cool. Cool! Cool! Cool!

(n)

(o) br ☆ Can You Guess My Magic Word? ☆

(p) Phone

(y) Classroom Rules
1. Quiet mouth
2. Quiet body
3. Eyes watching
4. Ears listening
5. Nice to others
6. Finishing my work
7. Doing my best!

(x) Question of the Day
How many days until our trip to the fire station?

(w) Little Bear Helpers

(z) Tooth Graph
Aug. Sept. Oct. Nov. Dec. Jan. Feb. Mar. Apr. May June July

(aa) Countdown
Look! Only
3
days left until
Our field trip!

(ee)

(bb) Dear Buddies in Room 2,
Today is Tuesday,
September 16, 2000.
We will paint with feathers today.

(cc) Do you like ☐?
🏀 basketball   ⛸ skating
Christina Anthony Bache   Chad   Josiah
Teri   Davis   Marty   Katy   David
Maria   Taylor   Eleni
Miles   Emma   Kristen

(dd) What Is The Weather Today?

There are a few basic displays that you will want to prepare before you begin to use your calendar on a daily basis.

Classroom Rules

Make a copy of the Classroom Rules reproducible, or invite the class to write their own set of rules, and post the list on the board. In the beginning of the year, you will want to read through the rules with your class on a daily basis. Then, as the year progresses, you may only need to review the rules on occasion.

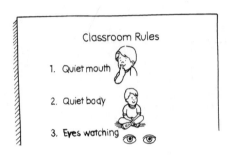

Helper's Basket

Cut a large rectangle from brown butcher paper to create a picnic basket. Cut a piece of white construction paper in half, write *Little Bear Helpers* on it, and glue it along the bottom of the rectangle. Make an enlarged copy of the Helpers reproducibles, and color each picture. Cut out the pictures, and glue four pieces on each of the remaining sides of the rectangle (as shown).

Laminate the basket, and staple the four corners to your calendar display. Staple a piece of fabric or colored construction paper over the top side. Twist a strip of brown butcher paper, and staple it above the rectangle to make a handle. Make enough copies of the Little Bear reproducible so that each student has a bear. Write each student's name on a bear. Cut out the bears, and invite students to color their cutout. Glue each cutout to a clothespin, and clip the cutouts to the top of the basket. Each day or week, choose eight students to perform the jobs listed on the basket, and clip their bear near their job title.

Materials
- Classroom Rules reproducible (page 10)

Materials
- Helpers reproducibles (pages 11–12)
- Little Bear reproducible (page 13)
- scissors
- brown butcher paper
- construction paper (assorted colors)
- glue
- crayons or markers
- stapler
- fabric (optional)
- clothespins

Alphabet Cards

Display a set of preprinted or handwritten alphabet cards across the top of your calendar display. Choose a set of die-cut shapes, or cut out your own. You will need 13 die-cuts of one color and/or shape and 13 of another color and/or shape (e.g., 13 blue kites and 13 green kites or 13 yellow suns and 13 white moons). Write a number from 1 to 26 on separate die-cuts of alternating colors (or shapes), and glue them in numerical order to the bottom corner of the alphabet cards. Use the alphabet cards described in the activities in this book (e.g., Alphabet Code on page 15), or create your own activities to help students learn letter recognition and alphabetical and numerical order.

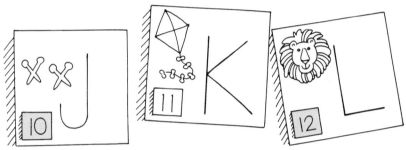

Good Morning Song

Teach students the song "Good Morning." Substitute the names of your students for the boldfaced names in the song. Laminate a copy of the song, and tape it to a paint stirring stick, a wooden dowel, or a ruler. Have students sit beside the calendar each morning, and point to each student when the class sings his or her name in the song.

Classroom Rules

1. Quiet mouth

2. Quiet body

3. Eyes watching

4. Ears listening

5. Nice to others

6. Finishing my work

7. Doing my best!

Helpers

Library Bear

Coat Bear

Paper Bear

Chair Bear

Helpers

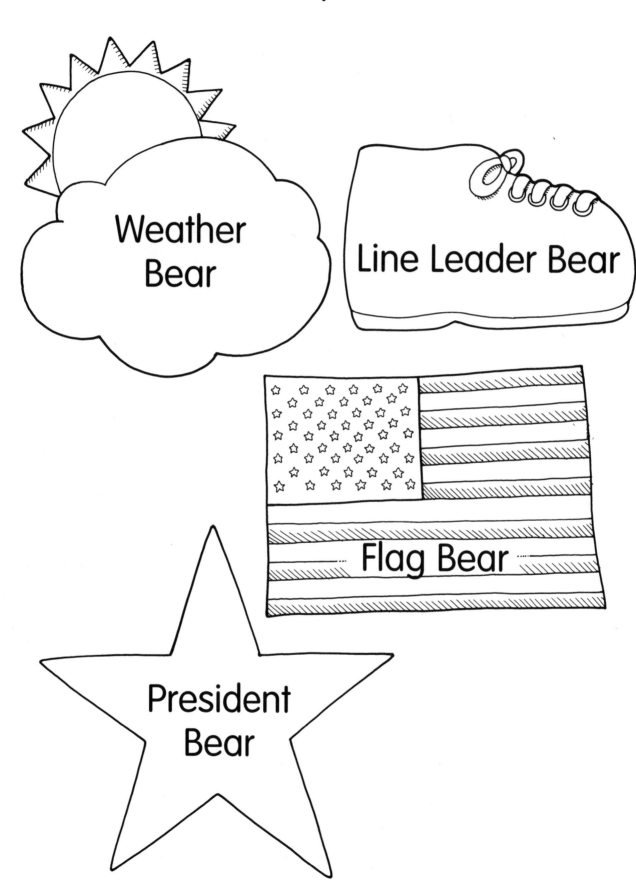

Weather
Bear

Line Leader Bear

Flag Bear

President
Bear

The Calendar and Beyond © 2000 Creative Teaching Press

Little Bear

Good Morning

(sing to the tune of "Good Night Ladies")

Good morning, **Dustin.**
Good morning, **Taeun.**
Good morning, **Cindy.**
We're glad you're here at school.

Good morning, **Kasha.**
Good morning, **Josh.**
Good morning, **Madeline.**
We're glad you're here at school.

14

Morning Message

This activity is a great way to introduce number, letter, and word recognition; dates; and grammar. Display a dry erase board on a chart stand or an easel. Place a set of dry erase markers near the board. Use one colored marker to write a message such as the following on the board:

> *Dear Buddies in Room 2,*
> *Today is Tuesday,*
> *February 6, 2001.*
> *We will cook a friendship salad today.*

In the beginning of the year, ask students to use a different-colored marker to circle the day of the week or familiar sight words in the message. Then, as students' skills develop, only write part of some of the words, and ask them to supply the missing letters, or insert grammatical errors into the message for students to correct. For example,

> *dear Buddies in Room 2*
> *Today is tuesday,*
> *February 6, 2001*
> *We will cok a friendship salad twoday.*

As the year progresses, feature longer messages and include more difficult editing problems.

Materials

- dry erase board
- chart stand or easel
- colored dry erase markers

Alphabet Code

Invite students to use the numbers written on the die-cut shapes that are taped to the bottom corners of the alphabet cards above the calendar to decode a secret message. Write *Can you read my code?* below the Morning Message on the dry erase board. Then, think of a word, and draw a line for each letter. Write the number for each letter of the word below the appropriate line. Invite student volunteers to write the letters that match the numbers on the coordinating lines to spell the mystery word.

Materials

- Morning Message display (see above)
- Alphabet Cards display (see page 9)
- dry erase markers

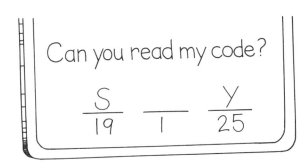

Days of the Week

Staple seven pieces of construction paper in a row above your calendar. Make a construction paper animal for each day of the week as follows: a snake for Sunday, a monkey for Monday, a toucan for Tuesday, a walrus for Wednesday, three tigers for Thursday, a frog for Friday, and a skunk for Saturday. Staple one animal above each piece of paper. Make a copy of the Ant pattern, and cut it out. Trace the pattern on construction paper to make five black ants and two red ants, and cut them out. Glue each ant to a rectangular piece of card stock. Write *Saturday* and *Sunday* on the backs of the red ant cards. Write the rest of the days of the week on the five remaining cards. Hole-punch the top two corners of each card, and pin the cards in order below the papers.

Use real food or construction paper to create the following dishes: white yarn and brown pom-pom balls to make spaghetti and meatballs for Sunday, real macaroni noodles for Monday, a brown circle stuffed with yellow and green paper shreds for a taco for Tuesday, a red semicircle with a rind cut from green paper and black beans glued on it for a watermelon for Wednesday, three wrapped Tootsie Rolls for Tuesday, fish crackers for Friday, and paper string beans for Saturday. Glue or staple each dish to a separate paper plate, and staple each plate next to the matching animal.

Materials

- *Today Is Monday* by Eric Carle (Scholastic)
- Ant pattern (page 28)
- stapler
- construction paper (assorted colors)
- scissors
- glue
- card stock
- hole punch
- straight pins
- white yarn
- brown pom-pom balls
- macaroni noodles
- dried black beans
- Tootsie Rolls®
- fish crackers
- small paper plates
- Wikki Stix

Use the Days of the Week display for the following activities:

- Explain to your class that each of these seven animals likes to eat something that starts with the first sound of its name on the day of the week that also matches the first letter of its name (e.g., spaghetti for the snake on Sunday). Each day, invite a student to turn over an ant card to reveal the word card for that day of the week. For example, on Wednesday, a student turns over the black ant below the walrus eating watermelon to reveal *Wednesday.* Tell students that the black ants represent the days that they go to school and the red ants represent the weekend.

- Invite students to sing "Today Is Monday," which appears in the back of the book *Today Is Monday.* Have students sing the song as written, or change the names of the foods to those featured in your calendar display.

- Invite students to look for words within words. Have them use Wikki Stix to circle words they find within the days of the week. For example, students could circle the words *We* and *day* in *Wednesday.*

Monthly Calendar Patterns

Cut a horizontal slit at the top of each square of a calendar. Insert a paper clip into each slit. Staple the calendar to the board. Write the name of the month on a sentence strip, or use a preprinted card, and staple it above the calendar. Staple a laminated copy of the song for that month near the calendar.

Choose two colors of a die-cut shape that coordinates with a theme for the month, such as red and pink hearts for February. Write the dates of the month on alternating colors of die-cuts to create an AB pattern on the calendar. Invite students to find the correctly numbered die-cut shape for that day and insert it in the paper clip. As the year progresses, vary the patterns (e.g., ABB or AAB), or introduce more colors to create more complicated patterns (e.g., ABC or AABBCC). After the activity, have the class sing that month's song.

Materials

- month songs (pages 29–40)
- Exacto blade
- calendar
- paper clips
- stapler
- sentence strips or preprinted month cards
- die-cut shapes

September

Sunday	Monday	Tuesday	Wednesday	Thursday	Friday	Saturday
	1	2	3	4	5	6
7	8	9	10	11		

"Write" Number of Days in School

Materials
- Number Writing Poems (page 41)
- dry erase markers
- dry erase board

Before you implement the number line activities described on the following pages, invite different students to write the total number of days they have been in school on a dry erase board. Read aloud the Number Writing Poems to help guide students as they form their numbers.

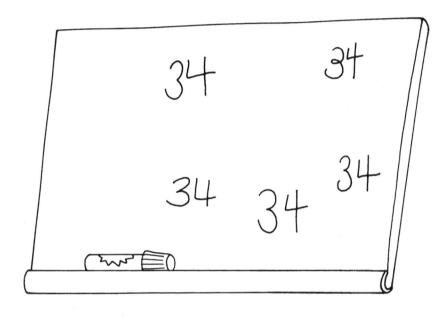

Rainbow Writing

Each day, use one of seven different-colored markers to write the number of days students have been in school on a strip of cash register tape that is displayed horizontally. Use a different color every day to create a pattern. After you write the first seven numbers, encourage students to predict the color of the marker you will use to write the eighth number.

8 9 10 11 12 13 14

red orange yellow green light blue dark blue purple

Patterned Number Line

Staple a long piece of cash register tape to your calendar display in a vertical line. Glue die-cut shapes to the number line to record the number of days in the year students have been in school. To begin, choose two different colors of one seasonal die-cut shape (e.g., colored apples). On the first day, write the number *1* on a red apple. On the second day, write the number *2* on a yellow apple. On the third day, write the number *3* on a red apple. As you write each number, read aloud the coordinating Number Writing Poem to help students focus on the procedure for writing that number.

To add interest, change the shape each month. For example, use pumpkins for October and leaves for November. As an option, tape photographs or printed pictures that represent special days (e.g., student birthdays, holidays, field trips) beside their corresponding numbers on the number line, and have the class sing an appropriate holiday song.

Materials

- Number Writing Poems (page 41)
- holiday songs (pages 42–47)
- stapler
- cash register tape
- glue
- die-cut shapes
- marker
- photographs or pictures (optional)

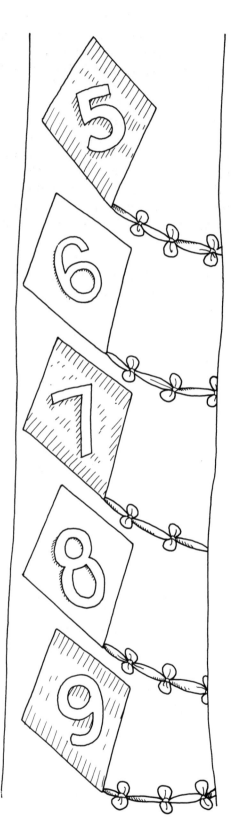

Tally Marks

Use a black marker to write *Tally Marks* on a sentence strip, and staple it to your calendar display. Staple a sheet of construction paper below the sentence strip and several sheets of blank white paper to the construction paper. Attach a dry erase board beside the *Tally Marks* sentence strip. Write *We Can Add (+) and Subtract (−)* at the top of the board.

Each day of the month, use a black marker to make a tally mark on the white paper. Use a red marker to circle each group of five tally marks. Each day, invite a few students to name an addition sentence for the number of tally marks they count. For example, on the twelfth day of the month, students could say *10 + 2 = 12, 8 + 4 = 12,* and *6 + 6 = 12.* Write each volunteer's number sentence and name on the dry erase board. As the year progresses, encourage students to write subtraction sentences, such as *13 − 1 = 12* or *15 − 3 = 12.*

This activity also provides a good opportunity to teach students about the communicative property. Explain to students that each addition sentence has a "buddy." For example, the buddy of the number sentence *5 + 2* is *2 + 5.* Or, teach students the additive property (i.e., any number plus zero equals that number, such as *4 + 0 = 4* or *6 + 0 = 6*). For students who have yet to grasp the concept of addition, an understanding of these properties will allow them to participate successfully in this activity.

Materials

- black and red markers
- sentence strips
- stapler
- construction paper
- white paper
- dry erase board

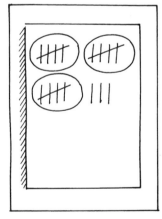

Tally Marks

We Can Add (+)
and Subtract (−)

$12 + 6 = 18$ Kyle

$6 + 12 = 18$ Louis

$19 − 1 = 18$ Teresa

$18 − 0 = 18$ Maki

Adding Up the Days of the Year

Make a copy of the Ones Chart. Cut out the word *tens,* and glue it to an empty Chinese food container (as shown). Staple the metal handle of the container to your calendar display. Cut out the word *ones* from the reproducible. Glue the rest of the page to the top of a piece of construction paper and the word *ones* below that. Staple the construction paper next to the container. Insert a straight pin through each of the ten dots on the reproducible. Place a straight pin below the Chinese food container and another one below the ones chart. Copy and cut apart two sets of Number Squares. Hole-punch each square, and place each set of squares on a metal ring. Flip the squares so that the number 0 shows on both rings. Place one ring on each of the pins below the Chinese food container and the ones chart. Place a container of linking cubes near this part of your calendar display.

Materials

- Ones Chart (page 48)
- Number Squares (page 49)
- scissors
- glue
- empty Chinese food container
- stapler
- construction paper
- straight pins
- hole punch
- metal rings
- container of linking cubes (2 colors)

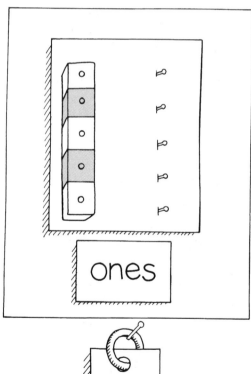

On the first day of school, invite a student to attach a linking cube to one of the pins on the ones chart. (Alternate the color of the linking cubes each day to create a pattern.) Ask students to count the number of blocks they see, and invite a volunteer to show that number on the ring of number squares below the ones chart. Each day, invite one student to add a linking cube to the chart and another to change the square on the ring to reflect the number of cubes. On the tenth day of school, prompt students to notice that there is no place on the ones chart to attach a cube. Show students how to attach the ten linking cubes in a pattern to make one stick. Place the ten-stick in the Chinese food container, and ask a student to find the card on the ring below that matches the number of ten-sticks. Ask a student to place a linking cube on the ones chart. Repeat the process daily, and encourage students to tell you when it is time to "trade" the linking cubes for a ten-stick.

Addition Game

Materials

- "Addition" song (page 50)
- Adding Up the Days of the Year display (see page 22)

Teach students the song "Addition" to help them learn their math facts. After the class sings the song, invite students to create a verse that shows an addition problem for the number of linking cubes from the Adding Up the Days of the Year display. For example, on the fifteenth day of the year, students might sing *10 + 5 is 15. 10 + 5 is 15. Adding is fun you know. 10 + 5 is 15.*

Penny Pinchers

Make a copy of the Our Piggy Bank reproducible, color it, laminate it, and staple it to your calendar display. Tack a plastic pocket onto the piggy bank. Tack another pocket beside it, and fill it with several quarters, dimes, nickels, and pennies. Attach a pad or stack of paper above the second pocket. Each day, invite a volunteer to select a combination of coins from the second pocket and place them in the pocket on the piggy bank to show how many days students have been in school. For example, a student could choose one nickel and two pennies on the seventh day of school. Remove the previous day's paper from above the coin pocket, and ask the student to write this amount and the ¢ sign on the top piece of paper. Teach the class the coin songs to help them learn the value of each coin.

Materials

- Our Piggy Bank reproducible (page 51)
- coin songs (pages 52–55)
- crayons or markers
- stapler
- thumbtacks
- clear plastic pockets
- pennies, nickels, dimes, and quarters
- pad or stack of blank paper
- pocket chart
- sentence strip
- index cards

To create a more challenging activity, replace the piggy bank display with a pocket chart. Write *Days in School* on a sentence strip, and place it in the top row of the pocket chart. Place four small pockets in the bottom row, and label them *25¢, 10¢, 5¢,* and *1¢*. Place quarters, dimes, nickels, and pennies in the corresponding pockets. Each day, invite five volunteers to each select a different combination of coins and place them in a row of the pocket chart to show how many days students have

been in school. For example, on the thirty-second day of school, one student could choose one quarter, one nickel, and two pennies and a second student could choose three dimes and two pennies. Ask one student to write this amount and the ¢ sign on an index card, and insert it beside the sentence strip at the top of the chart.

Odd and Even

Materials
- shoe box lid
- stapler
- sentence strip half
- container of linking cubes (2 colors)

On the inside of a shoe box lid, draw two rows of ten squares that are the same size as linking cubes. Label the ten squares on the bottom row *1, 3, 5, 7, 9, 11, 13, 15, 17,* and *19.* Label the ten squares on the top row *2, 4, 6, 8, 10, 12, 14, 16, 18,* and *20.* Staple the lid to your calendar display so that one edge of the lid forms a shelf. Write *Odd and Even* on a sentence strip half, and staple it above the lid. Place ten linking cubes of one color and ten of another color in a container near the board.

On the first day of the month, place a linking cube on the shelf so that it covers the square marked *1.* Tell students that this cube does not have a partner in the box above it so the number 1 is odd. On the next day, place a different-colored linking cube above the first one so that it covers the square marked *2.* Tell students that this cube has a partner in the box below it, so the number 2 is even. Repeat the process each day of the month, and encourage students to determine whether the number for the day is odd or even before you place the linking cube on the board.

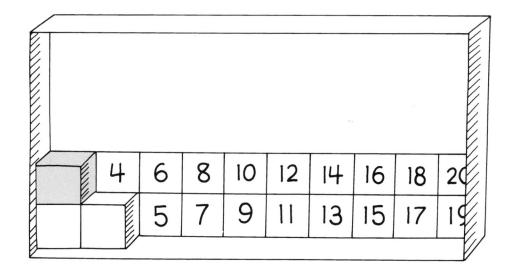

Daily Graph

Materials

- camera/film
- scissors
- glue
- colored index cards
- pocket chart
- sentence strips

Take a picture of each student, develop the film, cut out the pictures, and glue each one to a separate index card. Write each student's name below his or her picture, laminate the cards, and place them in the bottom row of a pocket chart. Write *Do you like* and *?* on sentence strip halves, and place them in the top row of the pocket chart. Each day, think of a simple question that pertains to something you are studying (e.g., *Do you like penguins or whales?*). Draw a picture or write the words for the two choices (e.g., *penguins* and *whales*) on separate sentence strip halves, and place them in the second row of the chart. Have students read the question on the chart first thing in the morning before calendar time starts and place their picture card in a pocket below their answer choice.

During calendar time, ask the class questions about the graph (e.g., *How many students like penguins?*). Then, invite students to help you determine the difference between the cards for both choices. Ask students to tell you which choice has more cards. Then, move cards one by one from the side with the most cards to the other side of the chart until the second column has the number of cards that the first one had. Ask students to count how many cards you moved, and explain that this number represents the difference between the two groups.

Do you like	?

⊛ basketball			🛼 skating	
Christina	Anthony	Bache	Chad	Josiah
Tori	Davis	Marty	Katy	David
Maria	Taylor		Eleni	
Miles	Emma		Kristen	

Daily Graph and Beyond

Change the look of your Daily Graph as the year advances. Write the question of the day (e.g., *Who is your favorite author?*) on a sentence strip, and place it in the top row of the pocket chart. Number separate index card halves from 1 to 10, and place them in descending order in separate pockets, starting with the one below the sentence strip. Write three or four possible answers (e.g., Eric Carle, Leo Lionni, and David Henkes) to the question on separate index card halves, and place them in the bottom row of the chart. Write each student's name on an index card half, and laminate the index cards. Have students read the question first thing in the morning before calendar time starts and place their name card in a pocket above their answer choice. During calendar time, ask the class questions about their graph (e.g., *How many more students like Eric Carle than Leo Lionni?* or *Do more boys or girls like David Henkes?*).

Materials

• sentence strips
• pocket chart
• index card halves

What is your favorite drink?			
10			
9			
8		Ashley	
7		Nicholas	
6		George	
5		Kim	Jenny
4	Kaitlin	Chloe	Sonja
3	Sammy	Miguel	Hitesh
2	Rick	Marcus	Lashieda
1	Nailah	Jamie	Kelsey
	milk	juice	pop

Sign Language of Colors

Choose a different color song each month, and staple it to your calendar display. Cut out a balloon from the same color of construction paper, and staple it above the color song. Make an enlarged copy of the Sign Language of Colors reproducible, cut out the sign for the corresponding color, and glue it on the balloon. Teach students how to make the sign, and invite them to demonstrate it as they sing the corresponding color song.

Materials

• color songs
  (pages 56–64)
• Sign Language
  of Colors
  reproducible
  (page 65)
• stapler
• scissors
• construction
  paper
  (assorted
  colors)
• glue

Ant

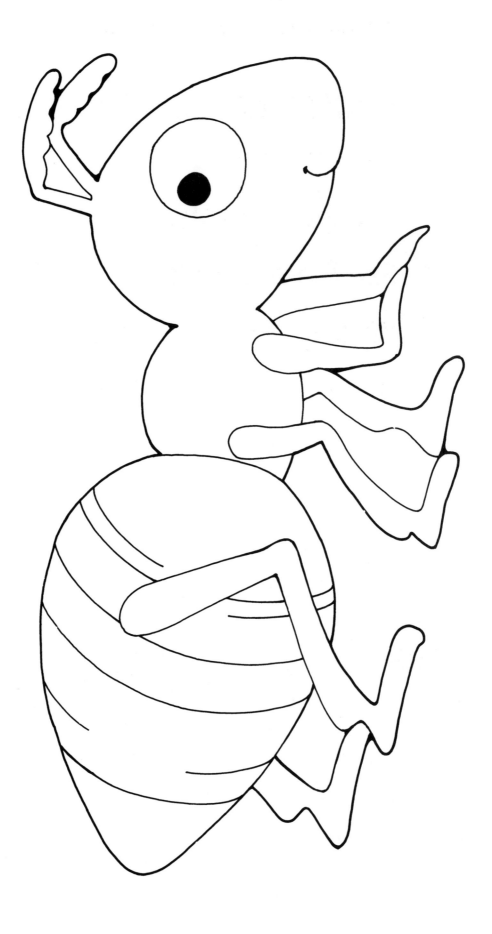

January

(sing to the tune of "Are You Sleeping?")

It is January.

It is January.

See the snowmen.

See the snowflakes.

What a time for skating!

What a time for sledding!

Winter's here.

Winter's here.

February

(sing to the tune of "The Hokey Pokey")

You put some red hearts here.

You put some pink hearts there.

You put some love in,

and you spread it everywhere.

You decorate a valentine

with glitter and a bow

For each of the friends you know!

March

(sing to the tune of "The Ants Go Marching")

The wind goes blowing through the town.

It's March! It's March!

Our hats go blowing all around—

In March! In March!

The wind makes the trees bend and sway.

And children fly their kites all day.

It comes in like a lion.

It goes out like a lamb.

We love to play in March!

March! March! March!

April

(sing to the tune of "I'm a Little Teapot")

I'm a little bunny, brown and white.

Can you see me hop to the left and right?

Every day of spring, I will say,

"Nibble, nibble, crunch!" and

Be on my way.

May

(sing to the tune of "Jingle Bells")

M-A-Y

M-A-Y

M-A-Y spells May.

Plants are growing.

Flowers bloom

In the month of May. Hey!

June

(sing to the tune of "I've Been Working on the Railroad")

I like playing in the summer

Outside in the sun.

I like playing in the summer.

Warm weather is such fun!

At the beach, I can go swimming.

At the park, I can fly my kite.

In June the days are so much longer,

And our day has more sunlight!

July

(sing to the tune of "Are You Sleeping?")

Firecracker,

Firecracker,

Sparkling bright

In the night.

Hear the boom and

watch the light.

See the colors.

What a sight!

Fourth of July!

Fourth of July!

August

(sing to the tune of "Bingo")

The month of August is so hot.
We love the sunny weather.
A-U-G U-S-T
A-U-G U-S-T
A-U-G U-S-T
Let's sing this song together.

September

(sing to the tune of "The Ants Go Marching")

It's time to come back to our school.

Hurrah! Hurrah!

It's time to come back to our school.

Hurrah! Hurrah!

We'll make new friends and learn

something new.

There's so much that we want to do

When we go back to school.

School is cool. Cool! Cool! Cool!

Octo

(sing to the tune of '

The little ghosts and goblins

trick-or-treat about.

They're looking for some candy,

we have no doubt.

Out comes the moon

that shines upon the lane.

Ring! goes a doorbell.

It's Halloween again!

November

(sing to the tune of "On Top of Old Smokey")

It is November.

The weather is fine.

You can see pumpkins growing

Up and down the vine.

Friends will gather together

For good food and great fun.

Their tummies will be full

When dinner is done!

December

(sing to the tune of "Jingle Bells")

Winter's here.

Winter's here.

Cold days all around.

Animals will hibernate

In burrows underground.

Winter's here.

Winter's here.

Let's all give a cheer.

Say good-bye to December—

The last month of the year.

Number Writing Poems

0   Round and round you go.
      Not too fast. Not too slow.

1   One is fun.
      Boop!

2   Around and back
      Down the railroad track. Choo! Choo!

3   Around the tree and around the tree—
      That's the way to make a three.

4   Down across and down some more—
      That's the way to make a four.

5   Jolly old five goes down and around.
      Put a hat on top—it looks like a crown.

6   Roll a hoop
      And make a loop.

7   Across the sky and down from heaven.
      That's the way to make a seven.

8   Make an s, but do not wait.
      Go back up, and close the gate!

9   A circle and a line
      Is the way to make a nine.

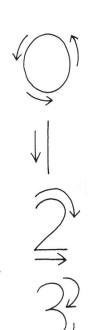
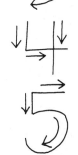

The Calendar and Beyond © 2000 Creative Teaching Press

Halloween

(sing to the tune of "Six Little Ducks")

Halloween pumpkins that I once grew.

Round ones, fat ones, tall ones, too.

But the one little pumpkin with the eyes

shining bright—

That is my favorite on Halloween night!

The Calendar and Beyond © 2000 Creative Teaching Press

Thanksgiving

(sing to the tune of "I'm a Little Teapot")

I'm a little turkey.
Look at me!
I'm as chubby
As can be.
You might think I'd be a
Tasty bite.
But I'll be hiding
On Thanksgiving night!

Mother's Day

(sing to your own tune)

I love you, Mom.
Yes, it's true.
I love you, Mom,
For all you do.
When I'm not with you
I'm blue.
Oh, Mom, I love you!

Martin Luther King Jr. Day

(sing to the tune of "Mary Had a Little Lamb")

Martin Luther wished for peace,

Wished for peace,

Wished for peace.

Martin Luther wished for peace

So we can live together!

Presidents' Day

(sing to the tune of "Old MacDonald")

George Washington was president

A long, long time ago.

He helped our country get its start.

And then he helped it grow.

Abe Lincoln was president

A long, long time ago.

He believed in freedom in his heart.

And then he helped it grow.

The Calendar and Beyond © 2000 Creative Teaching Press

St. Patrick's Day

(sing to the tune of "On Top of Old Smokey")

On top of a mountain,

All covered with green,

I met the sweetest leprechaun

I'd ever seen.

He wore tiny green boots

And a little black hat.

He gave me three wishes.

How about that?

Ones Chart

tens

ones

● ● ● ● ●

● ● ● ● ●

Number Squares

4	9
3	8
2	7
1	6
0	5

Addition

(sing to the tune of "The Farmer in the Dell")

1 + 1 is 2.
1 + 1 is 2.
Adding is fun you know.
1 + 1 is 2.

2 + 2 is 4.
2 + 2 is 4.
Adding is fun you know.
2 + 2 is 4.

$8 + 8 = 16$

3 + 3 is 6.
3 + 3 is 6.
Adding is fun you know.
3 + 3 is 6.

4 + 4 is 8.
4 + 4 is 8.
Adding is fun you know.
4 + 4 is 8.

$5 + 5 = 10$

5 + 5 is 10.
5 + 5 is 10.
Adding is fun you know.
5 + 5 is 10.

6 + 6 is 12.
6 + 6 is 12.
Adding is fun you know.
6 + 6 is 12.

7 + 7 is 14.
7 + 7 is 14.
Adding is fun you know.
7 + 7 is 14.

$3 + 3 = 6$

8 + 8 is 16.
8 + 8 is 16.
Adding is fun you know.
8 + 8 is 16.

9 + 9 is 18.
9 + 9 is 18.
Adding is fun you know.
9 + 9 is 18.

$4 + 4 = 8$

10 + 10 is 20.
10 + 10 is 20.
Adding is fun you know.
10 + 10 is 20.

Our Piggy Bank

The Penny

(sing to the tune of "Ten Little Indians")

What president is on the penny?

What president is on the penny?

What president is on the penny?

Abraham Lincoln!

How much is the penny worth?

How much is the penny worth?

How much is the penny worth?

A penny's worth one cent!

The Calendar and Beyond © 2000 Creative Teaching Press

The Nickel

(sing to the tune of "Mary Had a Little Lamb")

Here's a nickel I just found,

I just found,

I just found.

Here's a nickel I just found,

And now I have five cents!

The Dime

(sing to the tune of "Ten Little Indians")

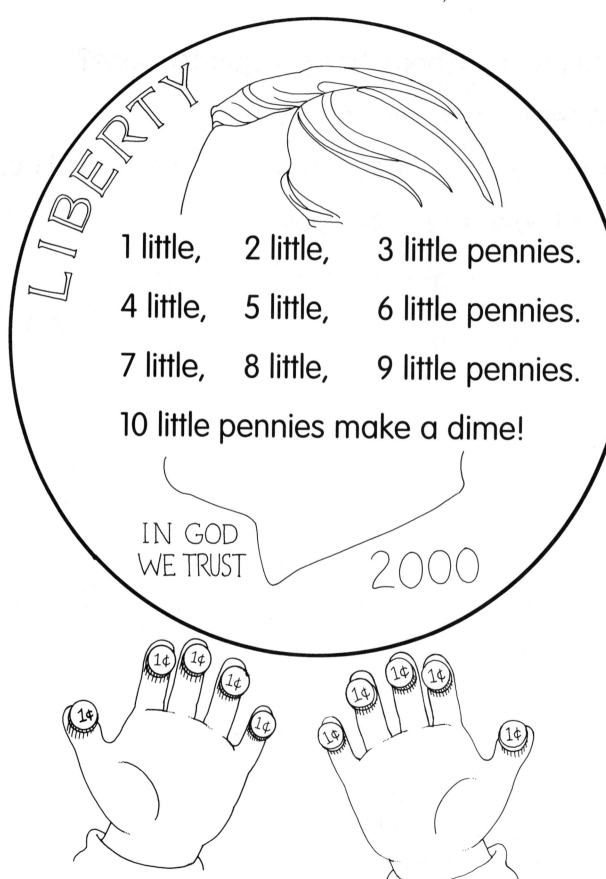

1 little,   2 little,   3 little pennies.

4 little,   5 little,   6 little pennies.

7 little,   8 little,   9 little pennies.

10 little pennies make a dime!

The Quarter

(sing to the tune of "Where, Oh Where, Has My Little Dog Gone?")

Where, oh where, has my quarter gone?

Where, oh where, can it be?

I've a hole in my pocket where 25 cents fell out.

And now I'm so unhappy!

Orange

(sing to the tune of "On Top of Old Smokey")

I like the color orange.

It makes me feel fine.

I love to see orange

All of the time.

Orange on flowers.

Orange on bugs.

Orange on carrots—

A food that I love!

Yellow

(sing to the tune of "Six Little Ducks")

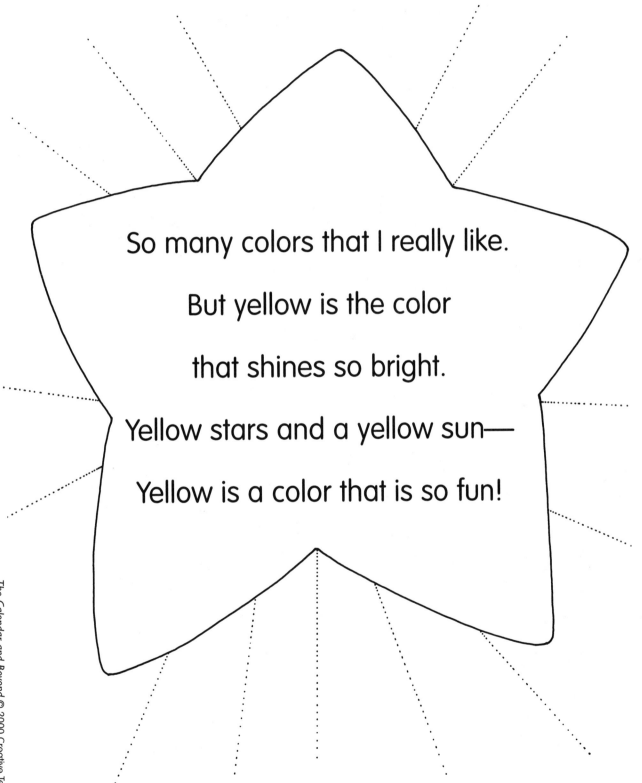

So many colors that I really like.

But yellow is the color

that shines so bright.

Yellow stars and a yellow sun—

Yellow is a color that is so fun!

Black

(sing to the tune of "I've Been Working on the Railroad")

I've been looking for black—
all day long.
I've been looking for black.
Would you like to come along?
I found it on a hat.
I found it on a bat.
I found it on a steam engine.
What do you think of that?

White

(sing to the tune of "Jingle Bells")

I like white.
I like white.
White is all around.
Oh, what fun it is to see
White snow on the ground!

I like white.
I like white.
White is all around.
Let us look around our room
To see where white is found.

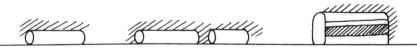

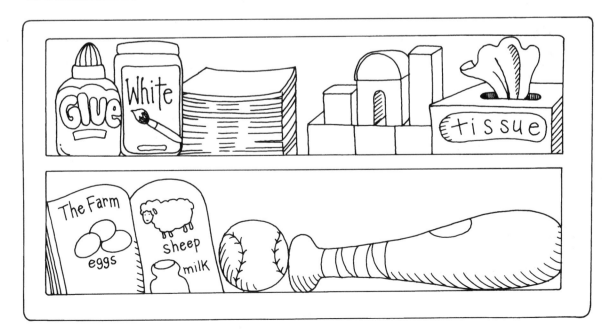

Red

(sing to the tune of "The Farmer in the Dell")

R-E-D
I like red.
Hi, ho! What do you know?
I like red.

Red is on my kite.
Red is on my bike.
Hi, ho! What do you know?
What red things do you like?

Blue

(sing to the tune of "Are You Sleeping?")

Where is blue?

Where is blue?

Here I am!

Here I am!

I am in the ocean.

I am in the sky.

I am in a blueberry pie,

A blueberry pie!

Purple

(sing to the tune of "Here We Go Round the Mulberry Bush")

Purple is one of my favorite colors,

Favorite colors,

Favorite colors.

Purple is one of my favorite colors.

I just mix red and blue.

red

blue

Brown

(sing to the tune of "The Itsy Bitsy Spider")

A little bit of brown is always around.

Down in the dirt is where it can be found.

Outside the squirrels are all wearing brown.

And so are the nuts

they are rolling on the ground.

Green

(sing to the tune of "The Bear Went Over the Mountain")

What do you think

green can be?

What do you think

green can be?

What do you think

green can be?

Let's take a look and see.

Green can be a bean.

Green can be a turtle.

Green can be a tree.

Oh, what do you think

green can be?

Look around and see!

Sign Language of Colors

Yellow

Black

White

Red

Blue

Brown

Green

Purple

Orange

Telling Time with a Sing-Song Rhyme

- Clock reproducible (page 76)
- crayons or markers
- scissors
- brass fastener
- stapler

Make an enlarged copy of the Clock reproducible, color it, laminate it, and cut out the face and two hands. Use a brass fastener to attach the hands to the middle of the clock, and staple it to your calendar display. When you first introduce the clock to your students, tell them to remember that the hour hand is the shorter hand because *hour* is a short word to say. (Say *hour* quickly.) Tell students to remember that the minute hand is the longer hand because it takes longer to say the word *minute*. (Say *minute* slowly.) Invite a student to stand beside the clock, and ask him or her to move the hands to show the hour that you name in the following song (sung to the tune of "The Muffin Man"):

> *Can you show what time it is?*
> *What time it is?*
> *What time it is?*
> *Can you show what time it is*
> *At* **six** *o'clock?*

Encourage the class to make a "ticktock" noise with their tongues after they sing. When the student at the board shows the correct time on the clock, tell the class to say *DING!* Choose a new student, change the bold-faced number in the song to name a new time, and repeat the activity.

Digital Time

Try this variation of the time-telling activity with late kindergarten and first grade students. Cut a rectangular piece of card stock, write *Hours* on the top left side and *Minutes* across the top right side, and draw a colon (as shown). Staple the rectangle below the clock. Make two sets of number cards for 0–9 on one color of index cards and one set of number cards for 1–12 on another color of cards. Hole-punch each set of cards, and place each set on a metal ring. Pin the rings for 0–9 under *Minutes,* and pin the ring for 1–12 below *Hours.* Repeat the Telling Time with a Sing-Song Rhyme activity, but encourage the student volunteer to also show the correct time on the digital clock.

Materials

- Clock display (see page 66)
- scissors
- card stock
- stapler
- colored index cards
- hole punch
- metal rings
- straight pins

Math Workouts

This activity encourages students to practice basic math skills in a way that is quick and fun. This is also a great way for students to warm up for a major math lesson. Cut two large rectangles from colored card stock, and glue them together on three sides to form a pocket. Write *Math Workouts* on the front of one rectangle, and use art supplies to decorate it. Laminate the pocket, make a slit in the unglued side, and staple it to your calendar display.

Write several simple math activities on separate index cards, and place them in the pocket. Examples of math workouts could include

- *Count to 5 then back to 1.*
- *Clap 10 times.*
- *Find 3 red things in the room.*
- *Count the number of hands in the room.*
- *Find things longer than your arm.*
- *Add the number of doors and clocks in the room.*
- *What is the next number after 4? 8? 9?*
- *Say "Math is fun!" 5 times.*

When you have a minute or two, pull out a card, read it aloud, and ask the class to perform that activity. Invite students to complete as many math exercises as time will allow.

Materials

- scissors
- colored card stock
- glue
- art supplies (e.g., markers, glitter, stickers)
- stapler
- index cards

Food Fractions

Write *Food Fractions* on a sentence strip, and staple it to your calendar display. Staple a colored plastic plate below the sentence strip, and attach several strips of Velcro to it. Make a copy of the food reproducibles, and color them. Laminate the pages, cut apart the pieces of each food item, and attach Velcro to each piece. Put all the pieces for each food item in a separate plastic bag. Choose a food item, and ask students to attach the number of pieces to the plate that shows a fraction that you name. Invite different students to show other fractional quantities. Use the pieces from other food items to repeat the activity.

Materials

- food reproducibles (pages 77–80)
- sentence strip
- stapler
- colored plastic plate
- Velcro
- crayons or markers
- scissors
- resealable plastic bags

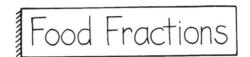

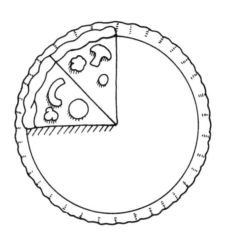

Ordinal Numbers

This simple idea is a great way to help students learn and practice ordinal numbers. Write the ordinal numbers for first through tenth (e.g., *1st, 2nd*) on separate paper squares. Staple the squares beside the calendar components you use daily in the order in which you use them. For example, place the square marked *1st* on the Morning Message board and the square marked *2nd* on the Days of the Week display. Invite students to use the ordinal numbers to tell you which activity will be next.

Materials

- small paper squares
- stapler

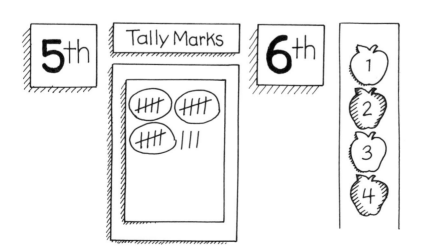

Can You Guess My Number?

Materials

• Numbers Chart (page 81)
• glue
• colored construction paper or card stock
• stapler
• scissors
• resealable plastic bag
• thumbtack
• sentence strip
• small sticky notes

Make an enlarged copy of the Numbers Chart, glue it to a piece of colored construction paper or card stock, and laminate it. Staple the laminated chart to your calendar display. Make another copy of the reproducible, and cut out all 50 squares. Place the squares in a plastic bag, and tack it to the display. Write *Can You Guess My Number?* on a sentence strip, and staple it above the chart. Draw an arrow on two separate sticky notes.

Invite a student to draw a number square (e.g., 34) from the bag, and ask him or her to show it to only you. Silently choose a range of seven or eight numbers (e.g., 30–36) that include the number, and place the arrow sticky notes so that they point to the first and last numbers in the range. Invite the class to take turns asking specific questions to help them identify the mystery number. For example, a student could ask *Is the number more than 31?* If the answer is yes, move the arrow to the left of 31 to the number 31. A student could also ask *Is the number less than 35?* If the answer is yes, move the arrow to the right of 35 to the number 35. Encourage students to continue asking questions, and move the arrows accordingly until they identify the mystery number.

The number is more than 23 and less than 26.

→	24	25	←	27
33	34	35	36	37
43	44	45	46	47

Solid of the Month

Cut a sentence strip in half, and write *Solid of the Month* on it. Glue the sentence strip to a piece of construction paper, staple it to your calendar display, and attach a piece of Velcro below the strip. Place a shoe box near the display.

Each month, select a different solid shape to explore with your class. Choose the shape (e.g., a cube), attach a piece of Velcro to it, and attach it to the piece of Velcro on the display. Discuss the properties of the shape (e.g., it has 6 sides or faces and it looks like a box), and have the class sing the coordinating shape song (e.g., "Square" on page 84). Invite students to bring small examples of the solid (e.g., dice or an empty jewelry box) from home to place in the shoe box. Share the contents of the box with the class, and encourage them to describe what they see.

Materials

- shape songs (pages 82–85)
- scissors
- sentence strips
- glue
- construction paper
- stapler
- Velcro
- shoe box
- small solid shapes (e.g., cube, cone, sphere)

Estimation Jar

Make an enlarged copy of the Estimation Jar reproducible, glue it to a piece of construction paper, and laminate it. Staple the laminated paper to your calendar display.

Use clear contact paper to attach a copy of the Estimation Jar Parent Letter to a jar or container, and fill it with manipulatives. Each day, invite a few students to guess how many of the items are in the container, and use a highlighter to write their estimations on sticky notes. Ask the students to trace their number and write their name on their sticky note and place it on the laminated estimation jar. Then, invite the class to sort the objects by color, shape, and other properties. Encourage students to arrange the items in groups of two, five, and ten and then count them. Invite the class to decide which number on the Estimation Jar display is closest to the actual number of items in the jar.

Have the student with the closest guess take home the container and fill it with a different quantity of small items. If the student with the closest guess has already had a turn to take home the jar, give the honor to the student with the next closest guess. Use a dry erase marker to write the number of items you would like in the jar on the blank line on the letter on the jar.

Materials

- Estimation Jar reproducible (page 86)
- Estimation Jar Parent Letter (page 87)
- glue
- construction paper
- stapler
- clear contact paper
- large plastic jar or container
- manipulatives (e.g., buttons, cotton balls, candy)
- highlighter
- sticky notes
- dry erase marker

Word Wall

Select a large area that adjoins your main calendar display to use as a word wall. Write each set of capital and lowercase letters of the alphabet (e.g., *Aa*) on a card stock square. Make 13 copies of the Honeybee reproducible, color the bees, cut them out, and laminate them. Glue each square (except those for the letters *w, x, y,* and *z*) and a honeybee cutout to a separate sheet of construction paper. Combine the squares for the letters *w* and *x* and *y* and *z*. Laminate all 24 pieces of construction paper, and staple the papers in alphabetical order to your calendar display in six rows of four. As an option, use a border to outline the word wall.

🐝 Aa am and	🐝 Bb by	🐝 Cc can	🐝 Dd
🐝 Ee	🐝 Ff for	🐝 Gg	🐝 Hh he
🐝 Ii	🐝 Jj	🐝 Kk	🐝 Ll
🐝 Mm me	🐝 Nn	🐝 Oo out of	🐝 Pp
🐝 Qq	🐝 Rr red	🐝 Ss she	🐝 Tt to
🐝 Uu up	🐝 Vv	🐝 Ww Xx was	🐝 Yy Zz zoo

Materials
- Honeybee reproducible (page 88)
- card stock squares
- crayons or markers
- scissors
- glue
- construction paper
- stapler
- preprinted border (optional)

Word Wall Words

Choose high-frequency words that coordinate with your curriculum, your current thematic unit of study, or students' interests. Only add words to the wall when students are watching so that you can discuss how the letters are formed, how the letters sound, and why the words are placed where they are on the wall. Use a black marker to write each word (e.g., *bag*) on a colored index card or a piece of construction paper. As you write each letter, describe for students its characteristics. For example, write a lowercase *b* and say B *is a blue sky letter because the top of the* b *goes to the sky. The letter* a *is a green grass letter because it stays on the ground, and the letter* g *is a brown dirt letter because the bottom of the* g *goes below the ground.* Cut out the word so that the shape of the letters is evident, and invite students to name the letter beside which the word should be taped. Repeat the activity with new words.

Materials
- black marker
- colored index cards or construction paper
- scissors
- tape

Word Wall Motivators

Materials

- curling ribbon
- bubble wands
- art supplies (e.g., glue, glitter, pom-pom balls)
- wooden dowels
- plastic glasses

Make a variety of props for students to manipulate or wear as they participate in word wall activities.
- Tie curling ribbon to a large bubble wand, or glue glitter and pom-pom balls to the end of a wooden dowel to create fun pointers.
- Pop out the lenses of inexpensive plastic glasses, decorate them with glitter and curling ribbon, and invite students to wear them as they read the words on the word wall.
- Make simple puppets, and encourage students to use them to point to the words as they read.

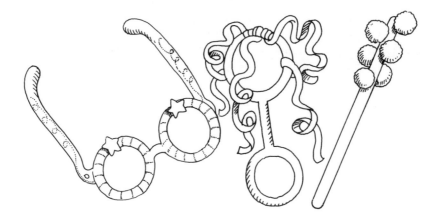

Three Cheers for These Words

Materials

- plastic pom-poms or mop heads

Invite four student volunteers to stand near the word wall. Give each student a pair of plastic pom-poms or mop heads. Read aloud a word from the wall, and invite the class to spell it. Ask the volunteers to move their arms as the class says the letters aloud. For example, say the word *pat*. As the class spells the word, invite the volunteers to move their hands to their sides for the letter *p*, to their chest for the letter *a,* and in the air for the letter *t*. Ask the class to spell the word three times as the volunteers move their arms. After the third spelling, encourage the class to shout out the word. Repeat the activity with a new word and volunteers.

Can You Guess My Magic Word?

Fold a large piece of construction paper in half horizontally. Write *Can You Guess My Magic Word?* on another piece of construction paper, and use art supplies to decorate it. Glue the paper to one side of the folded paper, and laminate it. Make a slit in each of the narrow ends of the laminated paper to create a sleeve. Staple the sleeve to your calendar display.

Cut paper strips that are a little narrower than the width of the laminated paper sleeve. Write a word on a paper strip, and slip it inside the sleeve so that only the first letter shows. (Reveal more than one letter if the first sound of the word is a blend or digraph, such as *shr* or *th.*) Invite students to make the sound of the letter or letters they see. Gently pull the strip to reveal the next letter or letters, and repeat the process. Continue to reveal letters one by one until students have blended all of the sounds to read the word correctly. Write a different word on a new paper strip, and repeat the activity.

Materials

- large pieces of construction paper
- art supplies (e.g., glitter, stickers)
- glue
- scissors
- stapler
- paper strips

Weather Wizard

Make several copies of the Weather Chart, hole-punch each page, and insert the pages in a three-ring binder labeled *What Is the Weather Today?* Place several crayons in a three-ring pencil case or resealable plastic bag, hole-punch the top, and insert it in the front of the binder. Hole-punch several sheets of blank paper, and insert them in the back of the binder. Every day, invite the student who has the job of Weather Bear (see Helper's Basket on page 8) to wear a decorated hat (optional) and record the weather for the day. Ask the student to color the next square beside the type of weather for that day on the chart and then write a sentence (e.g., *Today is sunny*), draw a picture, and write his or her name on a blank page in the back of the binder.

Materials

- Weather Chart (page 89)
- hole punch
- three-ring binder
- crayons
- three-ring pencil case or resealable plastic bag
- white paper
- decorated hat (optional)

Clock

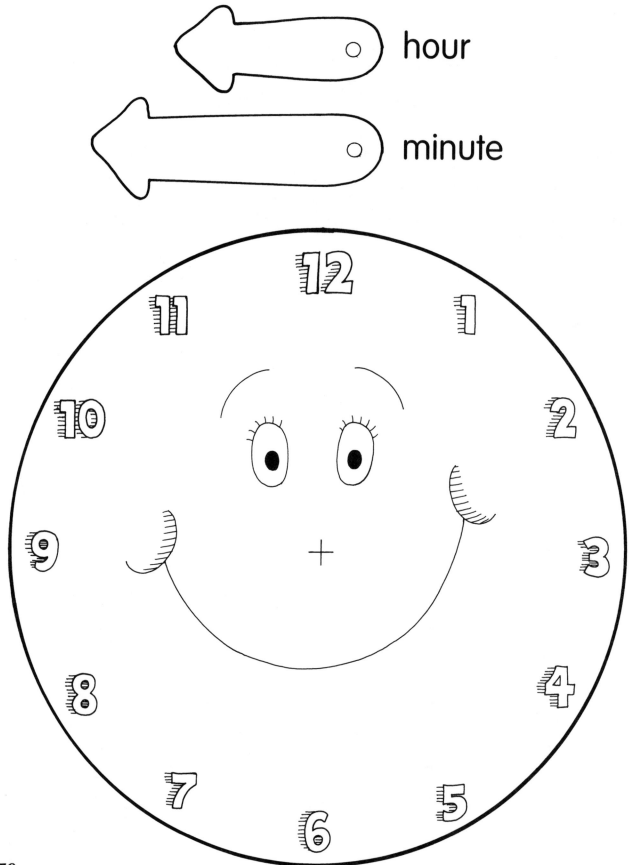

hour

minute

Orange

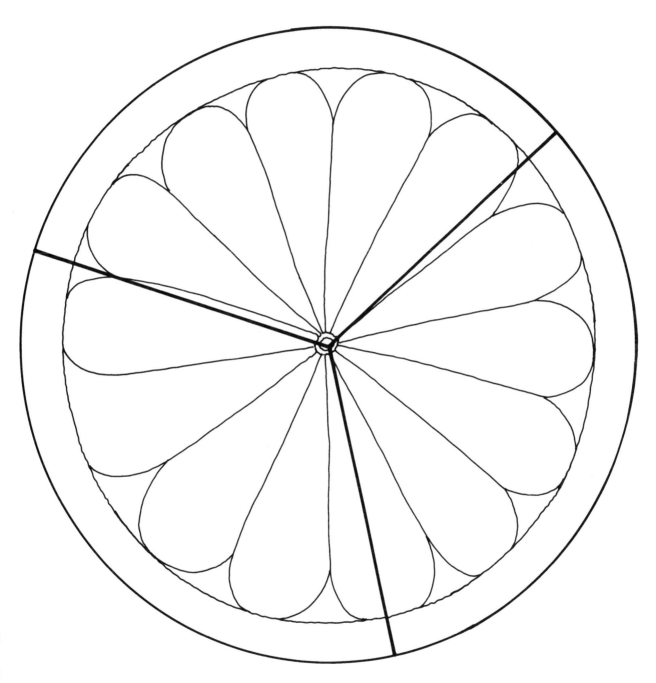

Sandwich

Pie

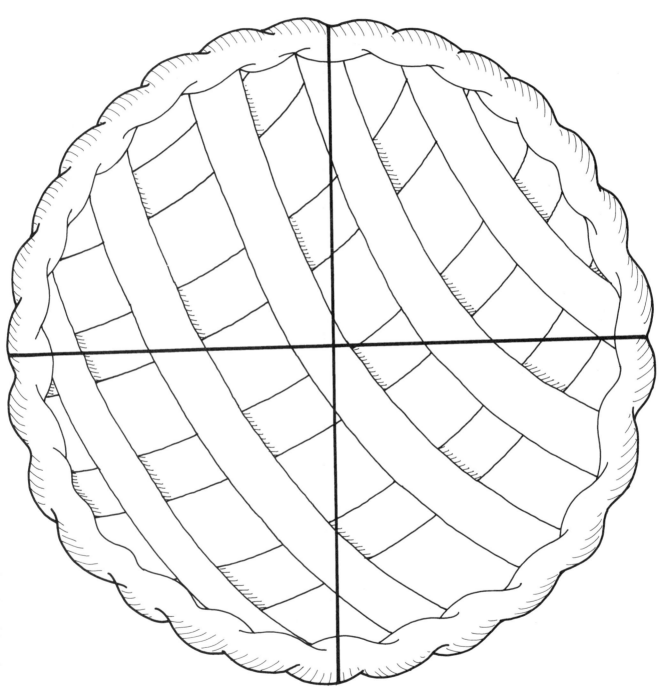

Pizza

Numbers Chart

1	2	3	4	5	6	7	8	9	10
11	12	13	14	15	16	17	18	19	20
21	22	23	24	25	26	27	28	29	30
31	32	33	34	35	36	37	38	39	40
41	42	43	44	45	46	47	48	49	50

Circle

(sing to the tune of "Are You Sleeping?")

I'm a circle.

I'm a circle.

Watch me bend.

Watch me bend.

I'm a curved line

That never ends.

I'm a circle.

I'm a circle!

Rectangle

(sing to the tune of "The Muffin Man")

Oh, do you know the rectangle?

The rectangle?

The rectangle?

It has two sides that are so long

And two sides that are short.

Square

(sing to the tune of "Three Blind Mice")

What am I?

What am I?

I have four sides.

They all are the same.

And that is something that

never will change.

Do you think you can

guess my name?

I'm a square.

I'm a square.

Triangle

(sing to the tune of "Twinkle, Twinkle Little Star")

I'm a triangle.
Yes, it's true.
I have three sides.
Yes, I do.
Count them with me—
one, two, three.
It's as easy as can be.
I'm a triangle.
Yes, it's true.
I have three sides.
Yes, I do.

Estimation Jar

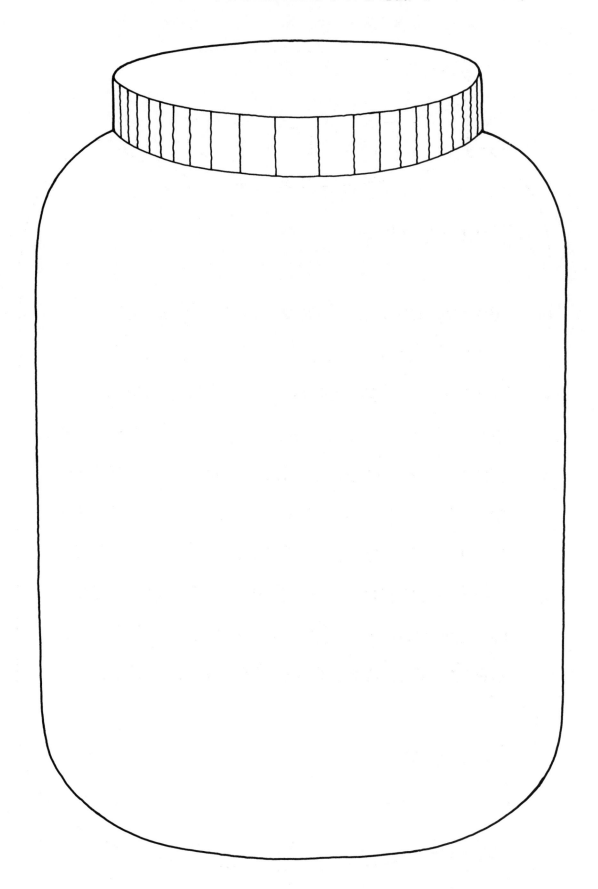

Estimation Jar Parent Letter

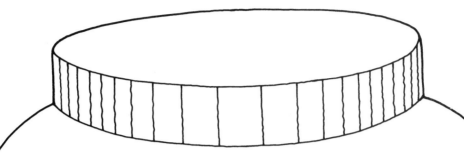

Dear Family,

We are learning how to estimate in school. Tonight your child is bringing home the Estimation Jar. Please fill the jar with no more than _____ of the same item. We will estimate how many items are in the jar. All edible items (please be sure that they are individually wrapped) will be shared with the class. All others will be returned home at the end of the week after they have been counted.

Thank you,

Honeybee

Weather Chart

sunny	windy	rainy	overcast	foggy	cold

Daily News

Materials
- drawing paper
- crayons or markers
- stapler
- folder
- bookbinding materials

Ask students *What did we do in school today?* or *What was your favorite thing that we did today?* to begin a discussion about the events of their school day. Choose an idea, and create a simple sentence for it, such as *Today we made lion puppets.* Invite students to whisper the sentence to their neighbor and then to their knee (yes, their knee). Then, ask students to tell you the first word in the sentence. Continue by saying things such as *The first word is "Today." How do we spell "to"? What kind of a "T" do we need to use since this is the first word of the sentence? Where can we look on the calendar to find out how to spell the word "day"?* As the students "coach" you, write the words of the sentence on a piece of drawing paper. Introduce and review the following skills as you write:

- Write the first word near the left margin.
- The first word in a sentence is always a capital letter.
- The names of people, places, months, and days of the week always begin with capital letters because they are special.
- Use one finger to make a space between two words.
- Choose a period, an "excited mark," or a question mark to end a sentence.

After you write the sentence, invite a student volunteer to illustrate it, and then staple it to the piece of construction paper below the animal for that day of the week (see the Days of the Week display on pages 16–17). At the end of the week, remove the illustrations, and place them in a folder. At the end of the month, bind the pages together to create a book titled *(Name of the Month) Daily News.*

Word Wall Revisited

Try one of these easy word wall activities to fill the last few minutes of the day and squeeze in some extra language practice.

- Silently choose a word on the word wall (e.g., *cat*). Say *I spy a word that rhymes with* **at**. Invite students to name a word from the word wall that rhymes with *at*. Encourage students to study the word wall carefully because there may be more than one word that rhymes with the word you named (e.g., *sat* or *that*). Change the boldfaced word of the sentence frame to a new word, and repeat the activity.

- Ask students to find words hidden in other words. For example, students could say that they see the word *row* in *grow*.

- Say *Can you guess my word? The first clue is that my word has* **three** *letters.* After students name all of the words on the word wall that have three letters, say *The second clue is that my word also has an* o. Encourage students to name every three-letter word on the word wall that has an *o* in it. Then, say *The last clue is that my word has* **two p's.** After students name the word (i.e., *pop*), choose a new word from the word wall, and change the boldfaced words and letters in the sentence frames to give three new clues.

- Give students practice identifying vowels and consonants. For example, say *My word has two vowels, and one of them is an* e or *Find a word with a consonant, a vowel, and a consonant.*

- Feature words in the same family (e.g., *sing, bring, thing*) on the word wall. Use glitter glue to write the rime (e.g., *-ing*) on pieces of construction paper, and invite students to name onsets (e.g., *s, br,* and *th*) that combine with it to make real words. Write each onset next to a rime.

Materials

- Word Wall display (see page 73)
- Word Wall Motivators (see page 74)
- glitter glue
- construction paper

Question of the Day

Write *Question of the Day* on a sentence strip half, and staple it to your calendar display. Write simple questions, such as *How much money is in our piggy bank today?* or *What number is between 15 and 17?*, on slips of paper. Place the strips in a resealable plastic bag, and tack the bag below the sentence strip half. Draw a strip, read aloud the question, and invite the class to give you the correct answer. Ask as many questions as time will allow before the last bell of the day rings.

Materials

- sentence strip half
- stapler
- slips of paper
- resealable plastic bag
- thumbtack

A Royal Guessing Game

Cut a paper crown from construction paper, and use a paper clip to fasten it into a circle. Each day, choose a student to act as the king or queen, and place the crown on his or her head. (Move the paper clip to adjust the size of the crown if necessary.) Write a word (e.g., *boat*) on an index card, and clip it to the front of the crown. Invite the class to silently read the word and then offer the king or queen clues as to what the word is. For example, encourage students to say things such as *Your word has four letters*, *Your word has two consonants and two vowels*, or *Your word rhymes with "coat."* Repeat the activity the following day with a new student and word.

Materials

- scissors
- construction paper
- paper clip
- index card

Photo Frieze Frame

This activity is a great way for students to get to know the faces and names of their classmates in the beginning of the year. Take a close-up picture of each student, and develop the film. Cut out rectangles from construction paper that are slightly larger than the pictures. Glue a student's picture to each rectangle, and write the student's name. Glue the name cards on sheets of construction paper (two cards per sheet). Arrange these sheets in a pile in alphabetical order. Cut out the capital form for each letter of the alphabet from a piece of construction paper, and glue each letter to a separate piece of a different color of construction paper. Attach a piece of heavy string or a clothesline across the room near the ceiling.

To assemble the "alphabet frieze," use clothespins to attach the paper with the letter *A* to one end of the string or clothesline, and all papers with student names that begin with *A* beside it. Repeat the process with the remaining letter papers and student name papers. Use a pointer to point to each letter of the alphabet and the name of each student that follows, and invite the class to join you as you read aloud the letters and names. For added fun, take pictures of class mascots and pets, and feature them in your alphabet frieze.

Materials
- camera/film
- scissors
- construction paper (assorted colors)
- glue
- heavy string or clothesline
- clothespins
- pointer

Mystery Objects

A visit from "Zero the Hero" every tenth day of school emphasizes the "magic" of the number ten. Hide a paper lunch sack filled with small treats somewhere in the room, and invite students to look for it. After a student finds the bag, invite the class to guess what is inside.

Draw a line down the center of a dry erase board. Label one column *Yes* and the other column *No*. Encourage students to ask questions about the shape of the objects in the bag (e.g., *Are they circles?* or *Are they squares?*). If the answer to the question is *no*, draw that shape in the *No* column. When a student guesses the correct shape, draw it in the *Yes* column, and invite students to ask questions about the color of the objects. Have students continue the process with questions about other physical characteristics, such as texture or size. After students correctly name the objects, invite the class to sort them (if possible), divide them into groups of five or ten, and then count the total number of items. At the end of the day, give each student one of the items, and place the leftovers in a prize jar.

Materials

- paper lunch sack
- small treats (e.g., inexpensive party favors, animal crackers, stickers)
- dry erase board and marker

Phone Numbers

Make an enlarged copy of the Phone reproducible, and cut it out. Glue the phone cutout to a piece of poster board, and staple it to your calendar display. (For an added touch, cut out ten squares from foam that match the squares for the numbers on the keypad, use puffy paint to write the numbers on them, and glue the foam "buttons" to the phone.) Bind 26 pieces of paper together into a class book titled *Class Phone Book.* Write the capital and lowercase form of each letter of the alphabet on a separate page. Write each student's name and phone number on the page that coordinates with the first letter of his or her name. For example, Aaron and Alicia and their phone numbers would appear on the page marked *Aa.* Place the class book near the phone display.

Ask a student to stand near the phone, and invite the class to sing "My Phone Number." At the end of the song, encourage the student to press the numbers for his or her phone number on the display as the class says the numbers aloud. If the student does not know his or her phone number, invite him or her to look it up in the class phone book. Then, invite the class to use the student's name to sing the following verse:

Paolo *knows his phone number,*
Phone number,
Phone number.
Paolo *knows his phone number.*
We are very proud!

Invite a different student to stand beside the phone display, and repeat the activity. For extra practice, place two phone cutouts and copies of the class phone book in a housekeeping center so that students can call each other.

Materials

- Phone reproducible (page 98)
- "My Phone Number" song (page 99)
- scissors
- glue
- poster board
- stapler
- foam and puffy paint (optional)
- bookbinding materials
- drawing paper

Let the Countdown Begin

Make a copy of the Countdown reproducible, and write the title of a holiday (e.g., Halloween or Valentine's Day) or a special event (e.g., Back-to-School Night or a class field trip) along the bottom. Glue the paper to a piece of construction paper, and staple a small pad or stack of paper to the middle of the construction paper. Staple the construction paper to your calendar display. Less than two weeks before the event, write down the number of days until the event on the top sheet of paper. Each day, invite a student to tear off the top page and write the next number in descending order.

Materials

- Countdown reproducible (page 100)
- glue
- construction paper
- stapler
- small pad or stack of paper

Left and Right

Fold a large piece of construction paper in half, trace your hand on the top, and cut through the folded paper to make two hands. Place the cutouts on a flat surface so that the thumbs touch. Write *left* on the first hand cutout and *right* on the second cutout. Staple the left-hand cutout to the top left corner of your calendar display and the right-hand cutout to the top right corner. Encourage students to refer to the hand cutouts whenever they need help determining their left from their right.

Materials

- large piece of construction paper
- scissors
- stapler

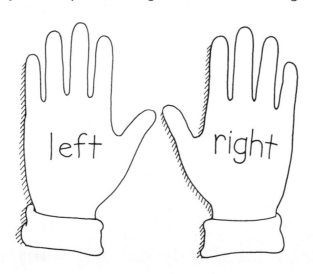

Patterns in Our World

Materials
• none

Explain to students that a pattern can be more than the example of alternating colors on the monthly calendar. Encourage students to notice and discuss the many patterns that occur in our world, such as night and day, the seasons, time on the clock, and the days of the week. For example, point to a component of your calendar display, such as the clock, and ask students to name the patterns that are associated with it. Students could say that the hour hand of the clock goes around the circle twice every day or that there are five minutes between each number on the clock.

Look Who Has Lost a Tooth!

Materials
• Tooth Graph (page 101)
• glue
• large piece of construction paper
• stapler
• light-colored crayons

Make an enlarged copy of the Tooth Graph, glue it to a large piece of construction paper, and staple it to your calendar display. Whenever students lose a tooth, invite them to write their name in a tooth above the current month and use a light-colored crayon to color the tooth. Occasionally, ask students questions about the graph, such as *How many students lost a tooth this month?* or *How many more students lost a tooth last month than this month?*

Tooth Graph

Aug.	Sept.	Oct.	Nov.	Dec.	Jan.	Feb.	Mar.	Apr.	May	June	July

Phone

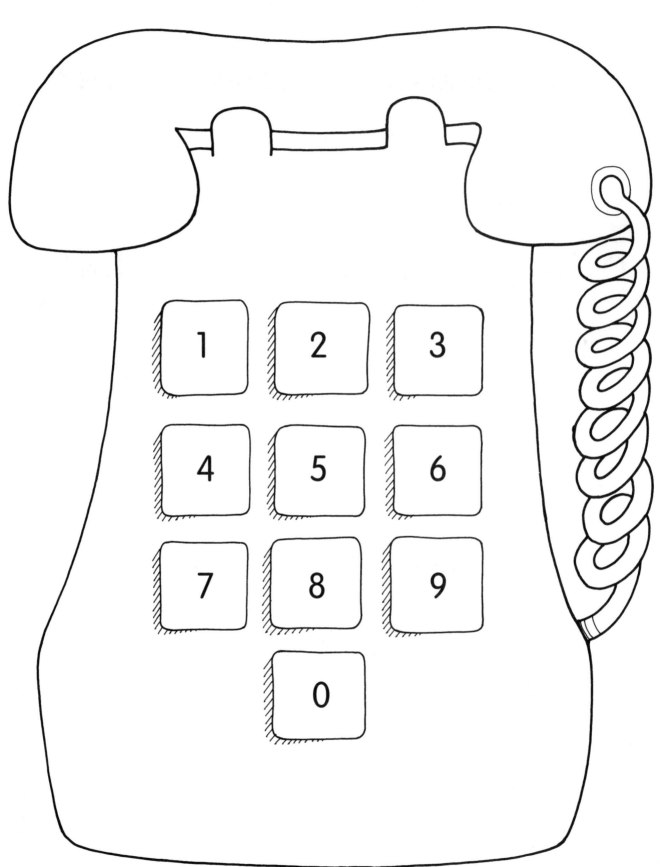

My Phone Number

(sing to the tune of "The Muffin Man")

Oh, do you know your phone number?

Your phone number?

Your phone number?

Oh, do you know your phone number?

Tell it to me now.

The Calendar and Beyond © 2000 Creative Teaching Press

Countdown

Look! Only

days left until

Tooth Graph

Aug.	Sept.	Oct.	Nov.	Dec.	Jan.	Feb.	Mar.	Apr.	May	June	July

Tooth Fairy Bag

Use fabric paint to decorate a canvas bag with a picture of a tooth and the tooth fairy and the title *Tooth Fairy Bag*. Make a copy of the Tooth Fairy Parent Letter, glue it to a piece of construction paper, and laminate it. Hole-punch the paper, insert a ribbon through the hole, and tie the ribbon to the handle of the bag. Hole-punch the book if it is a paperback, insert a ribbon through the hole, and tie the ribbon to the handle of the bag. (Otherwise, slip the book into the bag.) Place copies of the Tooth Fairy Journal and a resealable plastic bag of crayons or markers with holes punched at the top into a binder titled *Our Tooth Fairy Journal,* and then place the binder in the bag.

Invite students who lose their teeth to take home the bag. Encourage students to read the story with a family member and complete a copy of the journal page. Ask students to return the Tooth Fairy Bag to school the next day.

Materials

- *Where's Your Tooth?* by Rozanne Lanczak Williams (Creative Teaching Press), *The Tooth Fairy* by Sharon Peters (Troll), or *The Tooth Fairy* by Audrey Wood (Child's Play International)
- Tooth Fairy Parent Letter (page 103)
- Tooth Fairy Journal (page 104)
- fabric paint
- canvas bag
- glue
- construction paper
- hole punch
- ribbon
- resealable plastic bag
- crayons or markers
- three-ring binder

Tooth Fairy Parent Letter

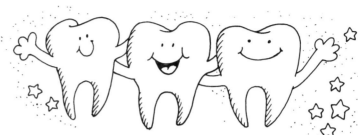

Dear Family,

Today your child lost a tooth! In honor of this special day, he or she brought home the Tooth Fairy Bag. Please help your child complete the following activities:

1. Read the tooth story.
2. Write a story and draw a picture in the Tooth Fairy Journal telling what you think the Tooth Fairy does with the teeth she collects.
3. Read your journal entry to someone special.
4. Return the bag to school tomorrow.

Have fun!

Tooth Fairy Journal

Dear Tooth Fairy,

I lost my tooth on

_____
(Date)

at _____.
(Place)

I think you use my teeth to _____

_____

_____.

Here is a picture of what I think you did with my teeth.

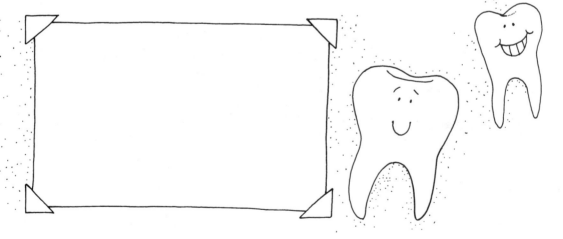

Love,

_____
(Your Name)

104

Apple Basket

Materials

- Apple reproducible (page 106)
- Apple Basket Parent Letter (page 107)
- colored paper
- scissors
- resealable plastic bag
- glue
- construction paper
- hole punch
- ribbon
- basket
- timer
- small dry erase board and marker or pad of paper and marker
- caterpillar puppet (optional)

Make 15 copies of the Apple reproducible on colored paper, and cut out the apples. Number the apples from 1 to 30, and laminate them. Place the apple cutouts in a resealable plastic bag. Make a copy of the Apple Basket Parent Letter, glue it to a piece of construction paper, and laminate it. Hole-punch the paper, insert a ribbon through the hole, and tie the ribbon to the handle of a basket. Place in the basket the bag of apple cutouts, a timer, a small dry erase board and a marker or a pad of paper and a marker, and a caterpillar puppet (optional).

Each day, invite a student to take home the basket and practice naming, ordering, and writing the numbers from 1 to 30. Explain to students that they should use the timer to see how many numbers they can name in a minute. Encourage students to practice putting the numbers into numerical order and writing them on the dry erase board or pad of paper. Remind students to return the basket to school the next day for another student to use.

Apple

Apple Basket Parent Letter

Dear Family,

Our little caterpillar likes to crunch apples for lunch! How fast can your child make the caterpillar munch?

We have been learning to name and identify our numbers from 1 to 30. Tonight your child has brought home the Apple Basket for practice with this skill. Please help your child complete the following activities:

1. Mix up the apple cutouts, and spread them over a table.
2. Use the timer to see how many numbers your child can recognize in a minute.
3. Help your child practice putting these numbers in numerical order.
4. Help your child practice writing each number.

Please return the basket tomorrow for another "Apple Muncher" to take home!

Sentence Suitcase

Materials

- Sentence Suitcase Parent Letter (page 109)
- index cards
- preprinted picture and word cards (optional)
- timer
- small suitcase
- art supplies (e.g., puffy paint, paint markers, glitter glue)
- glue
- construction paper
- hole punch
- ribbon

Copy words from your word wall onto separate index cards. Place these cards, preprinted cards that have one noun and a picture of the noun on them (optional), and a timer in a small suitcase. Use art supplies to decorate the suitcase, and label it *Sentence Suitcase*. Make a copy of the Sentence Suitcase Parent Letter, glue it to a piece of construction paper, and laminate it. Hole-punch the paper, insert a ribbon through the hole, and tie the ribbon to the handle of the suitcase.

Each day, invite a student to take home the Sentence Suitcase and practice reading the words on the cards to a family member. Encourage students to use the cards to make sentences. Challenge students to make as many sentences as they can in five minutes. Remind students to return the suitcase to school the next day for another student to use.

Sentence Suitcase Parent Letter

Dear Family,

Tonight your child has brought home the Sentence Suitcase. Your child knows many new words and has been practicing putting them together to make sentences. Please help your child make as many sentences as he or she can. Try using the timer to see how many sentences your child can make in five minutes. Encourage your child to read aloud each sentence to you.

Please return the suitcase tomorrow for another "Super Sentence Maker" to take home!

Honeybee Words Bag

Use fabric paint to decorate a canvas bag with a bee and the title *Honeybee Words*. Make a copy of the Honeybee Words Parent Letter, glue it to a piece of construction paper, and laminate it. Hole-punch the paper, insert a ribbon through the hole, and tie the ribbon to the handle of the bag. Make several copies of the Flower reproducible, cut out the flowers, write words from your word wall on separate cutouts, and laminate them. Place the cutouts, a small dry erase board and a marker or a pad of paper and a marker, and a bee puppet (optional) in the bag.

Each day, invite a student to take home the bag and practice reading words from the class word wall with members of his or her family. Encourage students to practice spelling the words aloud and writing them on the dry erase board or pad of paper. Remind students to return the bag to school the next day for another student to use.

Materials

- Honeybee Words Parent Letter (page 111)
- Flower reproducible (page 112)
- fabric paint
- canvas bag
- glue
- construction paper
- hole punch
- ribbon
- scissors
- small dry erase board and marker or pad of paper and marker
- bee puppet (optional)

Honeybee Words Parent Letter

Dear Family,

Help your child read these "honeybee words." The words written on the flowers are words we have been learning in class. Please help your child complete the following activities:

1. Place the flowers faceup on the floor. Tell your child to "buzz" over to a flower and read the word on it.

2. Have your child pick up the words that he or she reads correctly, and help him or her review any words that are left on the floor.

3. Ask your child to practice writing each word.

4. Have a buzzing good time!

Please return the bag tomorrow for another "honeybee" to take home!

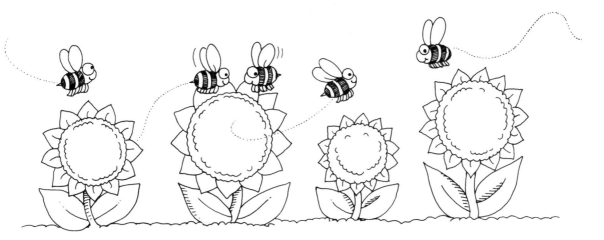

Flower